SPOT

FEELINGS

AFRAID

by Alissa Thielges

cry

sweat

Look for these words and pictures as you read.

wide eyes

hide

sweat

Tomas is scared to sing out loud.
He begins to sweat.

Peter is scared.
He does not like high places.
His eyes get wide.

wide eyes

cry

Ben has to get a shot.
He is afraid it will hurt.
He cries.

hide

Ada is afraid.
She hears a loud storm.
She hides.

It is okay to be scared. Sometimes facing your fears makes you stronger.

cry

sweat

Did you find?

wide eyes

hide

Spot is published by Amicus Learning, an imprint of Amicus
P.O. Box 227, Mankato, MN 56002
www.amicuspublishing.us

Copyright © 2025 Amicus.
International copyright reserved in all countries.
No part of this book may be reproduced in any form
without written permission from the publisher.

Library of Congress Cataloging-in-Publication Data
Names: Thielges, Alissa, 1995– author.
Title: Afraid / by Alissa Thielges.
Description: Mankato, MN : Amicus Learning, [2025] |
    Series: Spot feelings | Audience: Ages 4–7 | Audience:
    Grades K-1 | Summary: "What makes kids feel afraid?
    Encourage social-emotional learning with this beginning
    reader that introduces vocabulary for discussing feelings
    of fear with an engaging search-and-find feature"–
    Provided by publisher.
Identifiers: LCCN 2024017533 (print) | LCCN 2024017534
    (ebook) | ISBN 9798892000772 (library binding) |
    ISBN 9798892001359 (paperback) |
    ISBN 9798892001939 (ebook)
Subjects: LCSH: Fear in children—Juvenile literature. | Fear—
    Juvenile literature.
Classification: LCC BF723.F4 T48 2024 (print) | LCC BF723.
    F4 (ebook) | DDC 155.4/1246–dc23/eng/20240508
LC record available at https://lccn.loc.gov/2024017533
LC ebook record available at https://lccn.loc.
    gov/2024017534

Printed in China

Ana Brauer, editor
Deb Miner, series designer
Kim Pfeffer, book designer
and photo researcher

Photos by Dreamstime/
Seventyfourimages, 12–13; Freepik/
gelpi, 3; Getty Images/aldomurillo,
cover, Imgorthand, 6–7; Shutterstock/
Anatoliy Karlyuk, 1, Dragana Gordic,
8–9, kwanchai.c, 14, Zabavna, 10–11,
Zakharova_Elena, 4–5; Unsplash/team
voyas, 4–5